Why did people make mummies? How were pyramids built? What was the mysterious writing on mummy cases?

Unwrap the answers to these questions and more in . . .

Magic Tree House®
Research Guide
MUMMIES
AND PYRAMIDS

A nonfiction companion to
Mummies in the Morning

It's Jack and Annie's very own guide to the secrets of ancient Egypt.

Including:

- Hieroglyphic writing
- Egyptian gods and goddesses
- How mummies were made
- Tomb treasures and tomb robbers

And much more!

Here's what people are saying
about the Magic Tree House®
Research Guides:

The Research Guide is like the other half of the story. The facts make the adventure even more amazing.—Louis S., age 10

My eight-year-old son completed <u>Knights and Castles</u> in record time and loved every minute of it.—Claire G., parent

The Research Guides are perfect complements to the Magic Tree House books. —Cecelia D., parent

These guides are all teachers need to introduce nonfiction and research. —Donna J., media specialist

With the Magic Tree House Research Guides and the companion fiction titles, teachers have the perfect combination for teaching reading skills across the curriculum.—Lee Ann D., media specialist

Magic Tree House® Research Guide
MUMMIES AND PYRAMIDS

A nonfiction companion to
Mummies in the Morning

by Will Osborne
and Mary Pope Osborne

illustrated by Sal Murdocca

SCHOLASTIC INC.
New York Toronto London Auckland Sydney
Mexico City New Delhi Hong Kong Buenos Aires

No part of this publication may be reproduced in whole or in part, or stored in a retrieval system, or transmitted in any form or by any means, electronic, mechanical, photocopying, recording, or otherwise, without written permission of the publisher. For information regarding permission, write to Random House Children's Books, a division of Random House, Inc., 1540 Broadway, 20th floor, New York, NY 10036.

ISBN 0-439-31860-2

Text copyright © 2001 by Will Osborne and Mary Pope Osborne.
Illustrations copyright © 2001 by Sal Murdocca.
All rights reserved.
Published by Scholastic Inc., 555 Broadway, New York, NY 10012,
by arrangement with Random House Children's Books,
a division of Random House, Inc.
SCHOLASTIC and associated logos are trademarks and/or
registered trademarks of Scholastic Inc.

12 11 10 9 8 7 6 5 4 3 2 1   1 2 3 4 5 6/0

Printed in the U.S.A.   40

First Scholastic printing, September 2001

For Dr. Jack Hrkach

Historical Consultants:

EDITH WATTS, ELENA PISCHIKOVA, and DR. MICHAEL NORRIS, Metropolitan Museum of Art, New York, New York.

Education Consultant:

MELINDA MURPHY, Media Specialist, Reed Elementary School, Cypress Fairbanks Independent School District, Houston, Texas.

We would also like to thank Paul Coughlin for his ongoing photographic contribution to the series, and, again, our wonderful, creative team at Random House: Cathy Goldsmith, Joanne Yates, Suzy Capozzi, Mallory Loehr, and especially, our editor, Shana Corey.

MUMMIES
AND PYRAMIDS

Contents

Dear Readers,

We came back from our adventure in <u>Mummies in the Morning</u> with lots of questions.

Why did people make mummies? What was written in the Book of the Dead? How did ordinary people in ancient Egypt live?

We didn't go back to ancient Egypt to find the answers. We didn't even leave Frog Creek. We did <u>research.</u>

We started at the library. We found books about pyramids and mummies and a video about the Egyptian people. Then we checked the Internet. We found a site that told us more about ancient Egyptian writing. We took

lots of notes, and Jack drew a picture of a mummy's tomb.

Later, we watched a show on television about finding the tomb of a mummy called King Tut!

In this book, we're going to share our research with you. So get your notebook, get your backpack, and get ready to travel back five thousand years to learn all about mummies and pyramids.

Jack

Annie

1

Ancient Egypt

For thousands of years, mummies and pyramids were a great mystery. How were the pyramids built? Why did people make mummies? What was the strange writing on mummy cases?

In the last 200 years, scientists have learned a great deal about the people who built the pyramids and made mummies.

They were a hardworking people who enjoyed life. They loved science and music.

A person who studies ancient Egypt is called an Egyptologist (EE-jip-TOL-uh-jist).

A civilization is a group of people with an advanced way of life that includes science, art, and most often writing.

They believed in a sun god and a cat goddess. They thought they could live forever.

They were the people of ancient Egypt.

Egypt is where one of the oldest civilizations in the world began. Five thousand years ago, Egyptians invented one of the first forms of writing. They made a kind of paper from reed plants. They invented a calendar much like the ones we use today.

The ancient Egyptians built some of the most amazing buildings the world has ever known. Their painters and sculptors created beautiful works of art. Their doctors went to school to study how the body works.

Why did such a great civilization begin in Egypt so long ago?

14

Most historians think the answer is simple: the Nile River.

The Nile River is the longest river in the world. It flows through the middle of Egypt.

The Nile River flows into the Mediterranean Sea.

Egypt is located in northeast Africa.

The Nile gave the ancient Egyptians water for drinking and bathing. Egyptian fishermen caught many kinds of fish in the Nile. Hunters hunted wild birds along its banks. Boats sailed up and down the Nile, carrying people and goods.

But the Nile's greatest gift to the Egyptians wasn't fish or birds or drinking water or travel. It was mud!

The Sahara is the biggest desert in the world!

Floods and Farming

Most of the land in Egypt is part of the Sahara Desert. Desert soil is sandy and rocky. It is not good for farming.

The ancient Egyptians called the desert the Red Land. No one lived in the Red Land. Hardly anything could grow there.

The land along the banks of the Nile was very different from the Red Land. The soil there was dark and soft. The Egyptians called this land the Black Land. The Black Land was some of the best farmland in the world.

Why was the Black Land so good for farming?

Every July, the Nile flooded its banks. The floodwater dumped a layer of black mud along each side of the river.

The black mud was very *fertile* (FUR-tul). That means it was full of the things that plants need to grow.

In November, the floodwaters went down. Farmers plowed the Black Land. They planted seeds in the rich, fertile soil.

In March, they harvested their crops. The harvest was almost always very *plentiful*. That means there was more than enough food for everyone.

To harvest means "to gather and store the crops you've grown."

19

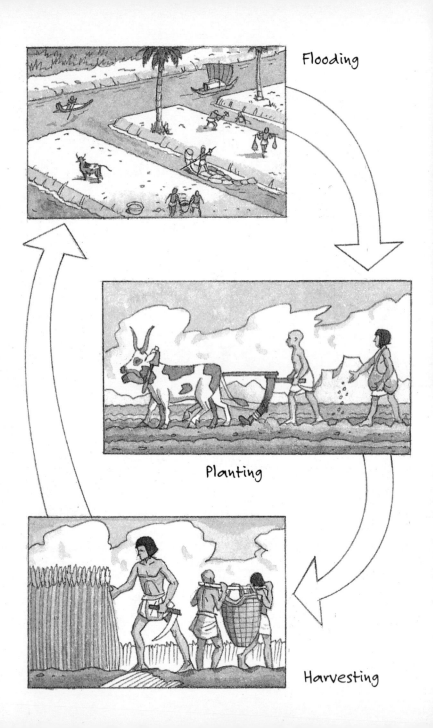

Flooding

Planting

Harvesting

Farm Year
July—flooding
November—planting
March—harvesting

Two Kingdoms

Villages formed near the good farmland along the Nile. Some of the villages became cities. Over time, the villages and cities became part of two separate kingdoms.

For many years, each kingdom had a different king. One king ruled over the land in the north, where the Nile flows into the sea. The other king ruled over the land in the south, along the Nile valley.

About 5,000 years ago, a king named Menes (MEE-neez) united the two kingdoms.

To **unite** means "to join together."

21

King Menes built a capital city close to where the separate kingdoms had met.

He wore a special crown. It was made from the crowns of both kingdoms.

Most historians say the joining of the two kingdoms was the beginning of the great Egyptian nation. When King Menes put on his double crown, he started a civilization that lasted for 3,000 years.

Turn the page to learn about the ancient Egyptian alphabet.

This Way

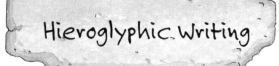

Hieroglyphic Writing

The ancient Egyptians wrote with pictures. Their picture writing is called *hieroglyphic* (HY-ro-GLIF-ik) writing.

The pictures were mostly of things from everyday life.

But the pictures did not always stand for the thing they showed.

Most Egyptians never learned to read hieroglyphs. There were over 700 different signs!

2

Everyday Life

Most ancient Egyptians were farmers. They lived in villages and towns in the Black Land along the Nile River. Their houses were made of mud bricks. The mud for the bricks was another gift of the Nile.

Even wealthy people lived in houses that were very close to each other. That's because Egyptians wanted to save most of the Black Land for farming.

Egyptian houses usually had high, flat

roofs. Families often did their cooking on the roof. They sometimes slept on the roof in the summer.

Poor families' houses usually had only one room. Wealthy Egyptians had larger houses. They had servants to do their cooking, washing, and other chores.

If you could peek beneath the roof of an Egyptian house, this is what you might see.

Most Egyptians did not have a lot of furniture. Their houses had only a few stools, small tables, and floor mats. Walls were painted bright colors. Ceilings were high to help keep the house cool.

Egyptians slept on beds made of wood and reeds. They rested their heads on headrests. The headrests were usually carved from wood.

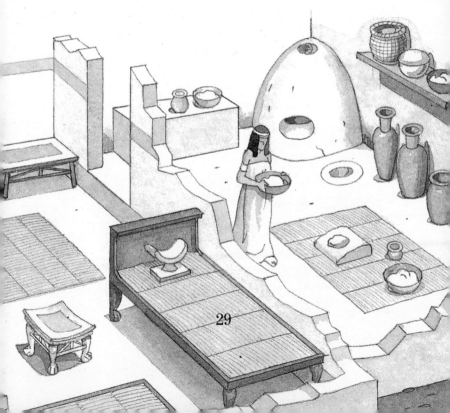

Climate means "the usual weather of a place."

Egypt has a very warm climate. Most ancient Egyptians hardly ever wore shoes. Their clothing was mostly white and loose-fitting. Almost all their clothes were made of *linen*. Linen is a cloth made from flax plants.

Ancient Egyptians cared a great deal about how they looked. Wealthy Egyptian men and women both wore eye makeup and wigs. They also wore necklaces, bracelets, and rings.

Egyptians loved perfume. They liked to rub good-smelling oils and creams on their skin.

Children and Family Life

Egyptologists believe the ancient Egyptians loved children. Egyptian art often shows parents having fun with their sons and daughters.

Yikes! Young children in Egypt didn't wear any clothes at all!

toy horse

Egyptian children played with spinning tops and balls. Both boys and girls played with dolls and wooden animals.

Children and grownups also played board games. These games were sort of like checkers or chess.

Tomb painting of an Egyptian queen playing a board game

Most children did not go to school. They lived with their parents until they were married.

Egyptian boys and girls wore their hair in a style called <u>sidelocks</u>. Nobody knows why.

The ancient Egyptians were some of the first people to keep animals as pets. The Egyptians loved their pets. They treated them like members of the family. One story says that when a family's pet cat died, the whole family shaved off their eyebrows to show their grief.

Artists and Craftspeople

There were many skilled artists and craftspeople in Egypt.

Sculptors and painters decorated the palaces and temples.

Potters worked with clay to make bowls, jars, and statues.

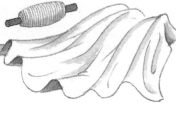

Weavers wove cloth for clothes and bedding.

A **barge** is a boat with a flat bottom.

Shipbuilders built sailboats and barges for traveling up and down the Nile.

Other craftspeople made leather goods and jewelry.

34

Egyptian Craftspeople

Sculptors and painters

Potters

Weavers

Shipbuilders

Leather workers

Jewelry makers

Egyptian craftspeople were very skilled at
their trades. They usually worked
together in large workshops, like this.

Scribes

One of the most important jobs in ancient Egypt was that of a *scribe*.

Scribes wrote on scrolls. These scrolls were made from a reed called <u>papyrus</u> (puh-PY-rus).

Scribes kept records for the government. They also kept records for merchants and traders. They copied down magic spells and scientific information.

It took years of schooling to become

a scribe. The hieroglyphic alphabet was very hard to learn. Most Egyptians never learned it at all. They hired scribes to read and write for them.

Not fair! Only boys could go to school and become scribes!

Pharaohs

The rulers of Egypt lived very differently from ordinary people. They had hundreds of servants. Their homes were grand palaces.

Egyptian rulers came to be called *pharaohs* (FAIR-roez). Pharaohs had total power over their people. Ancient Egyptians believed their pharaoh controlled the weather, the flooding of the Nile, and the growth of their crops.

Pharaoh means "great house."

Egyptians thought their pharaoh was more than a person. They worshipped him as a god.

Jack and Annie Present: The Animals of Ancient Egypt

Crocodiles, hippos, and beautiful birds lived along the Nile River. Lions, wild bulls, and jackals also lived in ancient Egypt. Egyptian statues and jewelry were often made to look like animals.

This glass fish held perfume.

This wooden goose sat on wooden eggs.

This lion guarded a jar of face cream.

This hippo was a good-luck charm.

3

~~~

Egyptian Religion

Ancient Egyptians worshiped their pharaoh. They also worshiped many gods and goddesses.

Egyptians pictured their gods and goddesses in several different ways. A few were like ordinary men and women. Some were like animals. Many were half-human and half-animal.

The Egyptians believed the gods and goddesses watched over everything they did.

41

Egyptian queen with falcon-headed god Horus

Temples

The Egyptians built great temples for their most important gods and goddesses. Inside the temples were sacred statues. Priests at the temples cared for the statues. They washed and dressed them. They even served them meals!

Ordinary people were not allowed to see the sacred statues inside the temples. When they visited, they said prayers and left gifts outside. At home, they prayed to their own statues of their favorite gods and goddesses.

The Next Life

An important part of Egyptian religion was belief in a *Next Life*. The Next Life was where people went after they died. There they could enjoy many of the same things they had enjoyed on earth.

Egyptians believed that every person was made up of three parts. The first part was the body.

The second part was the *ka*. The ka was the person's *life force*. It was what made the person alive.

The third part was the *ba*. The ba was what made the person different from anyone else.

Egyptians believed that when a person died, the ba and ka left the body. For the person to live in the Next Life, the ba and ka had to come together again.

Egyptians often showed the ba as a bird with a human head.

The body was home for the ba and the ka. So it was very important that the body of a dead person not be destroyed.

To keep the body from being destroyed, the ancient Egyptians turned it into a mummy.

Turn the page to learn more about the gods and goddesses of ancient Egypt.

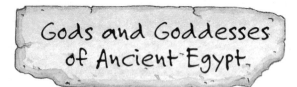

Gods and Goddesses of Ancient Egypt

Ancient Egyptians worshiped many gods and goddesses. Here are some of the most important ones.

RA (RAH)

Ra was the sun god. He was sometimes shown with the body of a man and the head of a falcon. The Egyptians believed Ra created the world. They thought Ra sailed across the sky every day in a golden boat. At sunset, Ra sailed his boat into the *underworld*. The underworld was a kingdom beneath the earth. At sunrise, Ra rose from the underworld and sailed his boat across the sky again.

OSIRIS and ISIS (oh-SY-ris and I-sis)

Egyptians believed that long ago, Osiris and Isis had been the first king and queen of Egypt. When Osiris was murdered by his evil brother, Isis used magic powers to bring him back to life.

Osiris became god of the dead and ruler of the underworld.

Isis became the goddess of healing, marriage, and motherhood.

HORUS (HOR-us)

Horus was the son of Isis and Osiris. He was a falcon-headed god. Egyptians believed their pharaoh was Horus in human form.

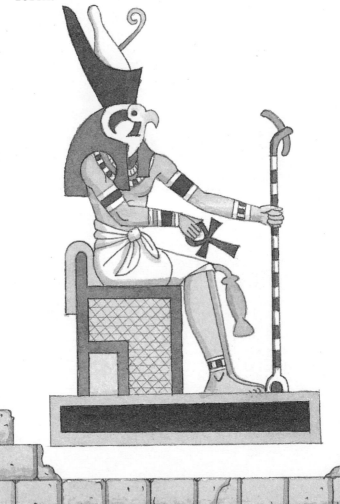

BASTET (BAST-ut)

Bastet was Ra's daughter. She was a cat goddess. She was shown as a cat, or a woman with a cat's head. Egyptians believed Bastet had the sun's power to make their crops grow. They prayed to Bastet for a good harvest every year. Bastet was also the goddess of music and dance and the goddess of joy and love.

THOTH (THOTH or TOTE)

Thoth was the moon god. Egyptians believed Thoth gave them the gift of writing. He was also the god of medicine and mathematics. He was sometimes shown as a baboon. He was also shown as a man with the head of a bird.

BES (BES)

Bes was one of the Egyptians' favorite gods. He was short, chubby, and happy. He had a lion's ears and tail—and the body and face of a man. Bes brought joy and good luck to families. He protected the whole household.

Nested mummy cases

4

Mummies

Normally, when an animal or a person dies, the body begins to *decay*. That means that the skin, hair, muscles, and other parts of the body start to rot away. Finally, there is nothing left but bones.

A *mummy* is a dead body that has been protected from decay.

The First Egyptian Mummies
The first Egyptian mummies were probably made by accident.

The ancient Egyptians needed the land near the Nile for farming. So they buried their dead in the nearby desert.

The hot desert sand dried out the bodies very quickly. They didn't decay. They became mummies.

The Egyptians studied these desert mummies. They learned from them how to protect the body for the Next Life.

Making a Mummy

It took a long time to make a mummy. The work was done by a team of priests. Egyptians believed the god Anubis (uh-NOO-bis) watched over mummy making. Anubis had the body of a man and the head of a jackal. So the chief priest wore a mask of a jackal.

The place where the priests worked was called the *Beautiful House*. Every-

Oh, wow! Egyptologists think that the ancient Egyptians made over 70 million mummies!

A jackal is a kind of wild dog that lives in Asia and North Africa.

thing in the Beautiful House was done with great care.

First, all the organs except the heart were taken out of the body. The ancient Egyptians believed that the gods weighed a person's heart when he or she tried to enter the Next Life. The weight of the heart would tell the gods if the person had lived a good life on earth.

Other organs were put in special jars to be buried with the mummy.

Next, the priests washed the body with wine. They said prayers. They rubbed the body with oils and spices.

Then the priests covered the body with a kind of salt called *natron* (NAY-tron). Natron worked like the desert sand, only better. It helped dry the body even more quickly and keep it from decaying.

Oh, man! The ancient Egyptians didn't know what a person's brain was for—so they threw it away!

Resin
(REZ-in)
is the sticky
stuff that
comes from
trees or
plants.

Finally, the priests laid the body on a slanted table. They said more prayers. Then they left the body to dry for about forty days.

When the body had dried out, it was wrapped in strips of linen. The linen had been soaked in resin. As they dried, the linen strips became very hard.

The priests wrapped magic charms in the mummy's linen strips. The Egyptians believed these charms would bring good luck and protect the person in the Next Life.

The priests wrapped and wrapped until the body was covered from head to toe.

Sometimes a mask of the person's face was placed over the linen strips. This was to help the ba and ka recognize the person underneath.

Some mummies were buried with more than a hundred charms!

The layer of linen strips on some mummies was several inches thick.

Sometimes the mummy's case was placed in a stone coffin called a <u>sarcophagus</u> (sar-KAHF-uh-gus).

When the body was fully wrapped, it was ready to be placed in its mummy case. There was usually a painting of the person's face on the mummy case, too.

Many mummy cases were decorated with paintings and writing. The paintings often showed the person entering the Next Life and meeting the gods. The writing spelled out prayers and magic spells.

Early mummy cases were rectangular boxes, like this one:

Later mummy cases were shaped
more like the mummy inside:

When the mummy was sealed inside
its case, it was ready to be taken to its
tomb.

**A tomb is a
burial place.**

Amulets

The magic charms wrapped in the mummy's linen strips are called *amulets* (AM-yuh-lits).

Some amulets were little statues of the gods.

Others were symbols, like a set of stairs leading to the Next Life.

Many amulets were in the shape of a beetle called a *scarab* (SKAAR-ub). The Egyptians believed that each day at dawn a giant scarab pushed the sun into the sky.

Scarab amulets were a symbol of rebirth in the Next Life. They often had wings.

Another very popular amulet is called the *Eye of Horus*. The Egyptians believed the god Horus lost his eye in a fight with his evil uncle. It was magically put back by the god Thoth.

Egyptians thought that Eyes of Horus painted on mummy cases would allow mummies to see outside!

5

~~~

Egyptian Funerals

Egyptian funerals were very big events. They were meant to send the dead person safely into the Next Life.

On the day a mummy was taken to its tomb, family and friends formed a *funeral procession*. The funeral procession was sort of like a parade.

The procession started at the dead person's home. It included family members, friends, priests, and servants.

To mourn means "to show sadness."

It was important to have a lot of people in the funeral procession. The dead person's family sometimes paid people to walk with them and mourn the person's death. These people might not have even known the person in life. But they would scream and cry and throw dust on themselves to show their grief.

If they did an especially good job of acting sad, they would be paid more!

The people in the funeral procession brought things they thought the dead person would need in the Next Life. They carried food and drink, weapons, tools, and musical instruments. If the person being buried was a child, they might even bring toys.

The funeral procession first went to the Beautiful House. There, the mummy in its mummy case was placed on a wooden barge. Oxen dragged the barge across the desert to the place where the mummy was to be buried.

As the procession crossed the sand, priests said prayers and recited magic spells. The ancient Egyptians believed it was important that everything be done

right, or the person would never get to the Next Life!

When the procession arrived at the tomb, there was a special ceremony. It was called "The Opening of the Mouth." A priest said a prayer. Then he touched the mummy's mouth. Egyptians believed the Opening of the Mouth ceremony made it possible for the dead person to eat, drink, and speak in the Next Life.

Finally, the mummy was ready to be laid in its tomb.

Turn the page to learn about
the Book of the Dead.

The Book of the Dead

Ancient Egyptians believed they would have to travel through the underworld to get to the Next Life. This journey was very dangerous!

To help them make the journey safely, mummies were buried with prayers, magic spells, and maps of the underworld. These prayers and spells and maps were called the Book of the Dead.

The Book of the Dead wasn't really a book. The spells and maps were written and drawn on papyrus scrolls.

The Egyptians believed that if the dead person followed the directions in the Book of the Dead and passed all the tests of the gods, he or she would live happily forever in the Next Life.

The Pyramids of Giza

6

The Age of Pyramids

Early pharaohs and other wealthy Egyptians had burial tombs made of mud bricks. These tombs are called *mastabas* (MAS-tuh-buhz). Mastabas looked like very large benches. They had flat roofs and slanted sides.

Mastaba is the Arabic word for "bench."

The mummy wasn't actually kept in the mastaba. It was buried underneath, in a room called a *burial chamber*. Sometimes the burial chamber was as much as eighty feet below the mastaba.

73

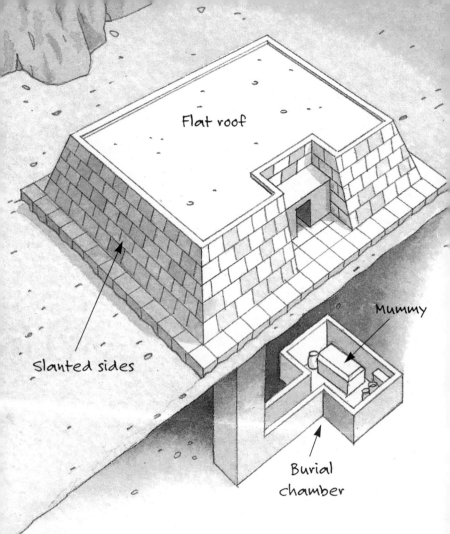

Flat roof

Slanted sides

Mummy

Burial
chamber

Mastabas were often built close to
each other. A group of mastabas
was called a "city of the dead."

The First Pyramid

The first pyramid was created by an Egyptian architect and priest named Imhotep (im-HO-tep).

An architect is a person who plans buildings.

Imhotep's pharaoh was King Zoser (ZO-sur). King Zoser wanted the most wonderful burial place that had ever been built. So Imhotep planned a giant stone mastaba for King Zoser. It would be the largest mastaba in all Egypt.

As the giant mastaba was being built, King Zoser decided he wanted something even better. Imhotep didn't know what to do. He started to make the stone mastaba bigger. Then he got another idea.

Imhotep decided to put a smaller mastaba on top of the first one. He put another mastaba on top of that—then another and another. Finally, Zoser's burial place was a stack of six mastabas.

Imhotep had created the first pyramid.

Imhotep's pyramid was nearly 200 feet high. After he died, the Egyptians worshiped Imhotep as one of their gods.

Imhotep's pyramid is called a step pyramid. It looks like a set of steps going up toward the sky.

Step pyramids were built for several pharaohs who ruled after King Zoser. Then Egyptians began to build another kind of pyramid.

The new kind of pyramid started as a step pyramid. But once it was built, the steps were filled in to make the sides smooth.

Some people think this smooth-sided pyramid was made to look like a ray of sunlight. It is the pyramid shape we know best today.

The Pyramids of Giza

The most famous Egyptian pyramids are the three smooth-sided Pyramids of Giza (GEE-zuh). They were built more than 4,500 years ago. All three are still standing today.

The largest of the Giza Pyramids is called the Great Pyramid. The Great Pyramid is nearly 500 feet tall.

 The Great Pyramid is the biggest stone building ever built!

The Great Pyramid was built for a pharaoh named Khufu (KOO-foo). In 1954, Egyptologists found a wooden boat buried near the Great Pyramid. The boat was over 140 feet long! They think it was probably the barge that led Khufu's funeral procession and carried his mummy to its tomb.

The base of the Great Pyramid would cover ten football fields!

Khufu's barge was made from over 650 separate pieces of wood!

Building the Pyramids

It took many years to build a pyramid. It also took thousands of workers.

Egyptologists think the workers used wooden rollers to move giant stones across the desert. Some of these stones weighed over 4,000 pounds!

No one really knows exactly how the workers put the giant stones in place. Most Egyptologists think they built large ramps to raise the stones up the sides of

the pyramid. When the pyramid was finished, the ramps were torn down.

Many people think the work on the pyramids was done by slaves. This is not true. Almost all the work was done by farmers during the flood season.

The farmers were paid to help build the pyramids. But most of them worked for a reason more important than money. They believed building the pyramids would help them get to the Next Life when they died.

The Great Sphinx

The Great Sphinx guards the Pyramids of Giza. A *sphinx* (SFINKS) is a make-believe creature with the body of a lion and the head of a hawk, a ram, or a person.

The Jack Sphinx!

The Great Sphinx has the body of a lion and the head of a pharaoh named Khafre (KAH-fray). King Khafre's pyramid is next to the Great Pyramid of King Khufu.

The Great Sphinx was carved from a rock mountain. It is the largest statue from ancient times still standing today.

7

~~~

Tomb Treasures and Tomb Robbers

The ancient Egyptians wanted to be as comfortable and happy in the Next Life as they had been on earth. So they filled their tombs with everything they thought they might need.

Mummies were buried with extra clothes and sandals, writing materials, and fans. Their families put makeup, wigs, combs, and mirrors in the tombs. They wanted the dead to look their best in the Next Life.

Mummies were even buried with food and drink for the Next Life. Bread, beef, figs, and jugs of beer have been found in their tombs.

Shabtis

Wealthy people wanted to have servants in the Next Life. Since they couldn't take their living servants with them,

they made servant statues. These statues were called *shabtis* (SHAHB-teez).

The Egyptians believed the shabtis would come to life—and go to work—in the Next Life.

There were often other statues in the tomb, too. Some were statues of the

Some shabtis had their own little mummy cases!

dead person. Egyptians believed these statues could be a home for the ba and ka if the mummy was destroyed. Other statues were there to guard the mummy and protect it from evil.

Tomb Robbers

The items buried with mummies could be very valuable. Many amulets, statues, and mummy cases were partly made of gold. Some were decorated with jewels.

The mummies' treasures were supposed to be used in the Next Life. But throughout history, many dishonest people have stolen the treasures to use in *this* life. These people are called *tomb robbers*.

When tomb robbers broke into a

Every pyramid standing today has been broken into by tomb robbers.

tomb, they took everything of value. They showed no respect for the mummy or its sacred resting place.

Tomb robbers broke open mummy cases. They took the amulets from the mummy's linen strips. They stole jewelry from the mummy's body. They took the makeup and perfume and body oils that had been left for the mummy to use in the Next Life.

Sometimes tomb robbers even burned the mummy to light the tomb while they worked.

Tomb robbing was very dangerous. Ancient Egyptians thought tomb robbers were committing crimes against the gods. If they were caught, they were beaten and often put to death.

Sadly, this did not stop others from robbing the mummies' tombs. Because of the tomb robbers' greed, many great treasures of ancient Egypt have been lost forever.

Tomb Paintings

One thing robbers couldn't steal was the art on the walls of a tomb. Tomb paintings have taught us a great deal about life in ancient Egypt.

Tomb paintings often show people dancing or playing musical instruments. It was believed the dancers and musicians in the paintings would dance, sing, and play for the dead person in the Next Life.

Tomb paintings also show the person who had died. Even if the person was old and weak at the time of death, tomb paintings show him or her as young and healthy. Egyptians believed that was how the person would live in the Next Life.

8

~~~

The Most Famous
Mummy of All

Pyramids were built to honor pharaohs and their families. But pyramids also told tomb robbers exactly where to look for treasure.

Pharaohs cared more about keeping their mummies safe than about having huge pyramids. So they began to build secret tombs they hoped robbers couldn't find.

The Valley of the Kings

The Egyptians called the Valley of the Kings the <u>Great Place</u>.

The Valley of the Kings is hidden deep in the Egyptian desert. It is surrounded by rocky cliffs with steep walls. There is a mountain near the Valley of the Kings that is shaped like a pyramid. The Egyptians thought this would be a perfect place to hide the tombs of their pharaohs.

94

The people who built tombs in the Valley of the Kings worked very hard to keep them hidden. They cut secret chambers into the rock. They dug passageways that led nowhere. They built false entrances.

They sealed the real entrances with heavy stones. Guards watched the tombs day and night.

Hidden Tombs

Secret chambers

Fake passageways

False entrances

Guards

Still, tomb robbers found the tombs—and their treasures. More than sixty royal tombs were cut into the cliffs in the Valley of the Kings. Tomb robbers found them all.

The Boy King's Tomb

For many years, Egyptologists searched the Valley of the Kings for the tomb of a pharaoh named Tutankhamun (TOOT-ahn-KAH-mun).

Tutankhamun is sometimes called the "boy king." He became pharaoh when he was nine years old. He died when he was only eighteen.

Egyptologists knew from ancient writings that Tutankhamun's mummy had been buried in the Valley of the Kings. But for years, no one had been able to find his tomb.

One Egyptologist who worked very hard to find Tutankhamun's tomb was Howard Carter. He searched for more than five years. He

Howard Carter

was about to give up—but then he made a discovery.

In 1922, Carter found stone steps buried beneath the ruins of some ancient workers' huts.

Could these steps lead to the boy king's tomb?

Carter and his team began to dig. The steps led to a door. Behind the door was a tunnel. They kept digging.

Finally, Carter and his team came to what they thought must be the entrance to a tomb. Carter broke a hole in the door. He held a candle and peered through the hole.

"What do you see?" called someone in Carter's team.

"Wonderful things," said Carter.

Carter saw gold everywhere he looked: gold statues, gold boxes, gold chairs.

In another room, Carter found a huge stone sarcophagus. When he opened it, he found a mummy case. Inside was a second

mummy case. Inside that was a *third* mummy case! The third mummy case was made of solid gold. And inside was the mummy of King Tutankhamun.

It took Carter and his team nearly ten years to study everything that was in Tutankhamun's tomb. The tomb had been broken into during ancient times, but very little had been stolen. The robbers had probably been caught before they could get away with much.

Cairo (KY-ro) is the capital city of Egypt today.

The tomb of Tutankhamun is the most famous mummy discovery of all time. Tutankhamun's treasures have been seen by millions of people all over the world. They are now in a museum in Cairo, Egypt—and King Tutankhamun's mummy is resting safely back in its tomb in the Valley of the Kings.

Turn the page to see some of the
treasures of Tutankhamun.

Jack and Annie Present: King Tut's Treasures

When Tutankhamun's treasures were shown in museums in America, the pharaoh was nicknamed "King Tut." Here are some of King Tut's treasures.

Ivory headrest

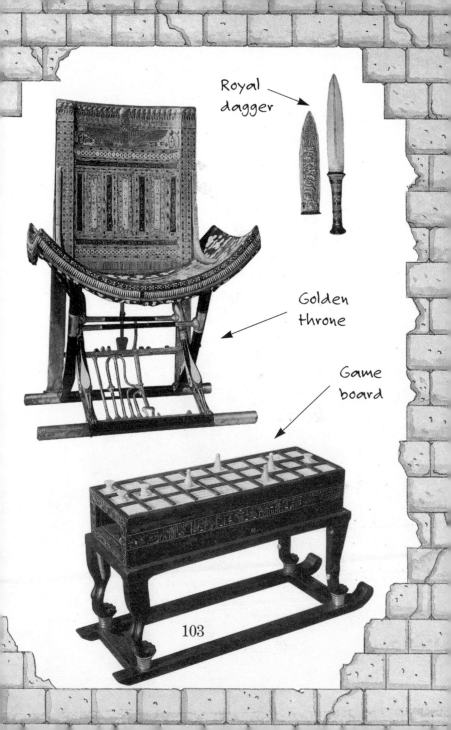

Royal dagger

Golden throne

Game board

103

9

Gifts of the Pyramids and Mummies

Each year, millions of tourists visit the ancient pyramids in Egypt. There are thirty-five pyramids still standing along the banks of the Nile River.

The pyramids are empty now. Their mummies and treasures are in museums all over the world. There, they are treated with great care and respect. Finally, they are safe from tomb robbers.

The mummies of Egypt have given us a great gift—the gift of knowledge.

The writings, paintings, and treasures of the mummies' tombs teach us how the ancient Egyptians lived, how they worked, and how they played.

This knowledge helps bring the distant past alive.

The ancient Egyptians believed they could live forever. In a way, they have.

Doing More Research

There's a lot more you can learn about mummies, pyramids, and the people of ancient Egypt.

The fun of research is seeing how many different sources you can explore.

Books

Most libraries and bookstores have books about ancient Egypt.

Here are some things to remember when you're using books for research:

1. You don't have to read the whole book. Check the table of contents and the index to find the topics you're interested in.

2. Write down the name of the book.

When you take notes, make sure you write down the name of the book in your notebook so you can find it again.

3. Never copy exactly from a book.

When you learn something new from a book, put it in your own words.

4. Make sure the book is <u>nonfiction</u>.

There are many books that tell make-believe stories about mummies. Make-believe stories are called *fiction*. Most stories about mummies are scary ghost tales. They're fun to read, but they're not good for research.

Research books have real facts and tell true stories. They are called *nonfiction*. A librarian or teacher can help you make sure the books you use for research are nonfiction.

Here are some good nonfiction books that tell the facts about mummies and ancient Egypt.

- *Ancient Egypt* by Judith Crosher

- *Ancient Egypt* by George Hart from the Nature Company Discoveries Library

- *The Ancient Egyptians* by Jane Shuter

- *The Egyptians*, Usborne Hotshots series, edited by Rebecca Treays

- *The Egyptians: Activities, Crafts, History* by Ruth Thomson

Museums

Many museums have statues, amulets, and even mummies from ancient Egypt. They often also have things the ancient Egyptians used in their daily lives. It's amazing to see things people used 5,000 years ago!

When you go to a museum:
1. Be sure to take your notebook!
Write down anything you see that catches your interest. Draw pictures, too!

2. Ask questions.
There are almost always people at a museum who can help you find what you're looking for.

3. Check the museum calendar.
Many museums have special events and activities just for kids!

Here are some museums around the country with good Egyptian collections:

- Brooklyn Museum of Art
  Brooklyn, New York

- Denver Museum of Nature and Science
  Denver, Colorado

- Field Museum of Natural History
  Chicago, Illinois

- Los Angeles County Museum of Art
  Los Angeles, California

- Metropolitan Museum of Art
  New York, New York

- National Museum of Natural History
  Washington, D.C.

- University of Memphis Institute of Egyptian Art and Archaeology
  Memphis, Tennessee

Videos

Most movies about mummies are *fiction*. There are some videos, though, that tell the real story of life in ancient Egypt.

Check your library or video store for these and other nonfiction videos:

- *Ancient Civilization: Egypt*
  from SVE & Churchill Media

- *Ancient Egypt*
  from Schlessinger Media

- *The Great Pharaohs of Egypt*
  from A&E Home Video

- *Mummies Made in Egypt*
  Reading Rainbow Video Episode 54
  from GPN Educational Media

CD-ROMs

CD-ROMs often mix facts with fun activities.

Here are some CD-ROMs that will help you learn more about ancient Egypt.

- *Egypt 1156 B.C.: Tomb of the Pharaoh* from Réunion des Musées Nationaux/ Canal+ Multimedia/Cryo Interactive Entertainment

- *Nile: An Ancient Egyptian Quest* (three-disk set) from Simon & Schuster Interactive

The Internet

Many Internet Web sites have facts about mummies and pyramids and the ancient Egyptians. Some even have games that help you learn more about these amazing people.

Ask your teacher or your parents to help you find more Web sites like these:

- touregypt.net
- www.clemusart.com/archive/pharaoh/ rosetta/index.html
- www.emory.edu/CARLOS/ODYSSEY/ EGYPT/homepg.html
- www.neferchichi.com

Good luck!

Index

Photos courtesy of:

VICTOR BOSWELL/NGS Image Collection (p. 79). **The British Museum** (front cover, pp. 32 top, 35, 36, 38, 39 bottom, 44, 60, 62 right, 62 left, 63 top, 63 bottom, 68–69, 86, 90, 91). **Paul Coughlin** (back cover). **Raphael Gaillarde/ Liaison Agency** (p. 32 bottom). **KENNETH GARRETT/NGS Image Collection** (pp. 66, 92, 94). **Hulton Getty/Liaison Agency** (pp. 19, 40, 70, 72, 82). **Michael Justice/Liaison Agency** (p. 78). **Kurgan-Lisnet/Liaison Agency** (p. 76). **The Learning Family Reisers/Robert Reiser © 1999/www.LearningFamily.com** (p. 104). **North Carolina Museum of Art/CORBIS** (p. 61). **Rainbird/Robert Harding** (pp. 31, 39 top, 39 center, 102, 103 top left, 103 top right, 103 bottom). **Walter Rawlings/Robert Harding** (p. 24). **© Photo.RMN** Reprinted with Permission from **Agence Photographique de la Réunion des Musées Nationaux** (p. 54). **Underwood & Underwood/CORBIS** (p. 96).

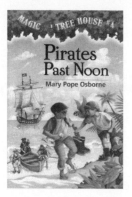

If you liked *Pirates Past Noon*,
you'll love finding out the facts
behind the fiction in

Magic Tree House®
Research Guide
PIRATES

A nonfiction companion to
Pirates Past Noon
It's Jack and Annie's very own
guide to pirates and their treasures!

Coming soon!

Calling all
Magic Tree House® readers!

Now you can discover the facts
about the exciting times and places
Jack and Annie visit with the

MAGIC TREE HOUSE®
RESEARCH GUIDES

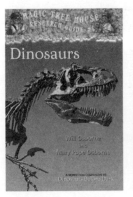
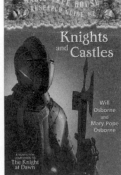
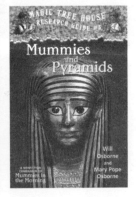

Look for them all!

MARY POPE OSBORNE and WILL OSBORNE have been married for a number of years and live in New York City with their Norfolk terrier, Bailey. Mary is the author of over fifty books for children, and Will has worked for many years in the theater as an actor, director, and playwright. Together they have co-authored two books of Greek mythology.

Here's what Will and Mary had to say about working together on *Mummies and Pyramids:*

"We had a great time doing the research for *Mummies and Pyramids*. The ancient Egyptians were an amazing people, and the more we learned about them, the more we wanted to know. We studied mummies, tomb paintings, and hieroglyphic writing at the British Museum in London, and we visited the Temple of Dendur at the Metropolitan Museum of Art in New York. Even though our book is finished, we've developed what we believe will be a lifelong interest in the civilization of ancient Egypt."